MBE'S GUIDE
TO
RAISING
CAPITAL

ISBN: 1456567594
EAN-13: 9781456567590
LCCN: 2011901269

MBE'S GUIDE TO
TO
RAISING
CAPITAL

ALONZO LLORENS

CHAPTER 1

Introduction

"Economic growth cannot be sustained without the inclusion of minority businesses and an infusion of capital into those businesses. Absent broad-based institutional investor participation in minority and immigrant business communities – soon to be the new majority of businesses – continued growth in the American economy is impossible, affecting not just minority businesses but putting the nation's macroeconomy at risk."

The Minority Business Challenge – Democratizing Capital for Emerging Domestic Markets, Milken Institute and Minority Business Development Agency (2000)

I begin this book with the above quote because it makes the point, in fairly stark terms, that our nation's long-term economic wellbeing hinges, to a large extent, on the success of minority business enterprises ("MBE"). Why is this the case? Primarily because in the not to distant future, minorities will become the new majority; therefore, as noted above, minority businesses will become the new majority. However, minority businesses have a long way to go before they are at a point where they can enjoy the level of economic growth that will allow them to become a fully functioning part of the engine that drives our nation's vast economy.

Indeed, there are several components that must fall into place before our minority businesses can expect to reach their growth potential. Nevertheless, in my opinion, there are two primary components that must exist above all else. First, minority businesses must become transformative in their thinking. By this, I mean, for example, that minority businesses must continue to strive to be (1) scalable, (2) in growth industries and (3) global in scope. Finally, minority businesses must be prepared and willing to obtain infusions of equity capital from the financial community.

While the need to become transformational is challenging enough, it is the financial component that seems to be the biggest challenge, which is why this book will attempt to demystify this issue as it relates to minority businesses. To this end, I will address the following. First, I will define minority business enterprise and its relevance. Second, I will discuss some of the preliminary steps that should be taken before seeking financing. Third, I will explain angel financing and its relevant aspects. Fourth, I will be discussing venture capital and its relevant aspects. Fifth, I will explain what is meant by a liquidity event, why it is important and discuss the different types.

My goal is to give you a snapshot of the business financing life cycle. What I've found, after practicing corporate law for over 20 years, is that many businesses don't have a solid grasp of the entire picture. For example, why should a business be concerned about properly forming a business today if it intends to raise multiple rounds of financing in the future. This book is not intended to give you a detailed breakdown of each component relating to the business financing life cycle. Instead, as noted above, it is intended to provide you with a solid overview of each component and, most importantly, provide you with a better understanding of how each of the pieces to the puzzle connect. With this information, I think you can better prepare yourself to be in position to raise capital and, hopefully, be better positioned to reach your greatest potential.

CHAPTER 2

Minority Business Enterprise

One of the threshold issues to be considered when forming a company is whether it should be designated as an MBE. Moreover, why is it important to make such a determination? Let's begin with this latter issue first (i.e., why is it important to determine whether your company qualifies as an MBE). Being designated an MBE can have the following implications:

- It may help position your company to gain business with companies who are desirous of utilizing the services of MBEs. For example, if designated as an MBE, the company may be eligible to generate business with large majority corporations as a result of its supplier diversity programs. As I mentioned in the *Introduction*, I believe that minority businesses must continue to be transformative in their thinking. Encompassed within this is the need to have a scalable business as many of these large majority corporations are looking for scalable MBEs to do business with.

- It may allow you to become eligible for certain financing opportunities. For example, there are loan programs at the federal, state and local levels that are specifically designed for MBEs.

National Minority Supplier Development Council

On its face, one might think that as long as a minority forms the company, runs the company or has a controlling interest in the company, then it is, in fact, an MBE. Well, not so fast. While these are all contributing factors in determining whether a company is an MBE, they are not in and of themselves determinative. While there are several qualifying agencies and entities that are in existence, the primary organization in this regard is the National Minority Supplier Development Council ("NMSDC"), which is a national organization that provides a direct link between corporate America and minority businesses. Specifically, NMSDC is a national organization that was formed in 1972 to provide increased procurement and business opportunities for minority businesses of all sizes. There are regional councils throughout the country that help carry out NMSDC's mandate. In order to become a member of NMSDC, an entity must be certified as an MBE by one of the affiliated state entities. For example, if your company is set up to do business in the State of Georgia, you would go to the Georgia Minority Supplier Development Council for certification. Of course, in order for an entity to be certified as an MBE, it must first meet the definition of an MBE. The NMSDC's definition of a "minority-owned business," which is the litmus test used by most organizations, is the following:

1. the company must be a for-profit enterprise (regardless of size),

2. physically located in the United States or one of its territories and

3. is owned, operated and controlled by minority group members.

The phrase "minority group member" is defined by the NMSDC to include "United States citizens who are Asian, Black, Hispanic and Native American." Ownership by minority individuals is deemed by the NMSDC to mean a business that is "at least 51% owned by such individuals or, in the case of a publicly-owned business, at least 51% of the stock is owned by one or more such individuals. Further, the management and daily operations are controlled by those minority group members." Although it will be discussed later in the book, it should be noted here that the NMSDC has recently introduced its Growth Initiative that puts into place a set of standards for MBEs that are currently certified and seek an infusion of equity capital but gives them the opportunity to potentially maintain their MBE status.

Governmental Agencies

As discussed throughout this book, there are certain governmental agencies at the federal level, in particular, that play an important role as it relates to the facilitation of economic growth in the minority business community. The primary agency is the U.S. Department of Commerce, which is where the Minority Business Development Agency ("MBDA") is housed. The MBDA is the only governmental agency created specifically to foster economic growth within the minority business community. Importantly, the MBDA has established a Strategic Growth Policy designed to create a model that facilitates sustainable businesses of size in growth industries.

CHAPTER 3

Preliminary Steps to Take Before Seeking Financing

To some degree, a company's ability to obtain equity capital begins long before it actually attempts to raise funds. Indeed, in my opinion, a company's ability to successfully raise capital hinges to a large extent on what occurs before the company is even formed and the initial decisions that are made once the company is formed. This normally boils down to the following critical areas: (1) professional service providers, (2) business plan, (3) management team, (4) choice of entity and (5) MBE considerations.

Professional Services

To begin, I truly believe that it is important to hire an attorney and hopefully an accountant as you prepare to form your company. Some of the primary reasons I believe this is important are set forth below.

First, I can't tell you how many times a company has hired me to represent it as it seeks to raise capital only to find out that the organizational documents, among other things, were not properly drafted. As a result, I have to revise the appropriate documents such that the company is best positioned to raise the capital it is seeking. This can present problems on a couple of fronts. First, it can potentially delay the offering, which is some instances may be time sensitive. Finally, if a potential investor is aware that these issues exist, then it may leave a negative impression.

Second, if you anticipate raising capital once the company is formed, then your attorney and/or your accountant should be a resource for you in terms of potential funding sources. The reason for this is that venture firms and most angel investors receive a large number of business plans on a daily or weekly basis. These potential investors have neither the time nor the desire to read each and every business plan that lands on their desk. Therefore, many of them will rely upon professionals they trust to do some of the initial vetting for them. So, if you don't have a network of potential funding sources that you can reach out to, then this is something your service providers should be able to help you with. This is a value-add that your attorney and/or your account can provide for you.

Finally, these service providers can give you invaluable advice with respect to your business plan. They've likely seen enough business plans such that they know a good one when they see it. Moreover, they know what the investment community looks for when it reviews a business plan.

Business Plan

The importance of your business plan cannot be overstated. In addition to being your blueprint for success, it is the first opportunity that a potential investor will have to make an informed judgment about the potential viability of your business model. Your business plan should be well thought out, polished and present your business model in a clear and cohesive manner. To do this, I believe that it is important that you, the business owner, write the plan. I see far to many instances where the business owner will hire someone to draft the plan, because they don't think they have the ability to do so. Well, there are a few things that are worth pointing out in this regard. First, if you take the time to write out your business plan the first thing it will do is allow you to see where the holes are in your business model. Writing a business plan forces you to think through issues. If you put in the proper effort behind your business plan, you will be surprised at how it allows you to fine tune your business model. Second, as a general matter, your business plan should include 3-5 years of projected financial statements. This is where it's helpful to have an accountant in place because if your business plan does not have financial projections that are remotely reasonable then you can lose credibility. Once again, if someone else is writing your business plan, then there is always the potential that your financials do not tie in accurately to the business model. Finally, if you really do believe that your writing skills are not strong enough for you to develop a polished business plan, then I urge you to write as many drafts as possible on your own first. Then, once you've taken it as far as you can take it, you send it to a professional writer to polish-up the business plan.

Now that I've hopefully convinced you to write your own business plan, the next question you're likely asking is what information should be contained within it. To some degree, there is neither a right nor a wrong way to draft a business plan. However, I do recommend that your business plan contain the following components at a minimum:

1. **Executive Summary** – While you hope that anyone receiving the business plan will take time to read the entire document, such that they have a complete understanding of your business, this is not always the case. This is why having a polished and precise executive summary is critically important. First, if someone does not have time to read the entire document, this person will, at least, have a very good concept of the business. Also, if someone is reading the executive summary, it can be a determining factor in terms of whether that person goes on to read the remainder of the document.

2. **Business** – Your business plan is, in part, about telling a story and it is here that you should set forth your business model. At a minimum, the business section can be broken down into the following parts:

   a. *Background* - This is essentially a summary section that provides a succinct description of the business and the industry it's in.

b. *Company* – This section will describe in detail the business your company is in.

c. *Industry* – This section should provide a detailed overview of industry you will be in.

d. *Sales and Marketing* – This section will describe the strategy that will be employed to separate your product or service from the existing market, thereby putting you in the best position to maximize your sales.

e. *Competition* – This section will describe your competition and how your business intends to compete with them.

f. *Intellectual Property* – This section will describe any intellectual property the company has.

g. *Regulations* – This section will describe any government regulations that are particularly germane to the company's operations.

h. *Property* – This section will describe any property the company either has or intends to purchase and its location.

i. *Employees* – This section will set forth the number of employees, if any, the company has.

3. **Management Team** – Management, management, management to business is what location, location, location is to real estate. Depending upon the investor, if the management team isn't the first thing looked at it is certainly the second. Irrespective of the order, however, a solid management team is imperative. The business

plan should identify each senior executive officer along with that person's position and background. The background description should generally cover a five year period and it should set forth any boards the officer sits on along with that person's educational background.

4. **Board of Directors** – A solid board slate is also very important. It conveys to a potential investor that other seasoned business leaders have bought into your business model and have committed themselves to make it work. Each board member should be identified and that person's background should be described in the same manner as the management team.

5. **Board of Advisors** – It is not imperative that you have a board of advisors. Generally, a company will select a board of advisors if they are in a highly technical area, and it wants to enhance it potential source of advisors. If you do elect to have a board of advisors, then they should be identified as well and described in the same manner as the management team and board of directors.

6. **Principal Stockholders** – It is very important that you have a clear and concise beneficial ownership section, because this will set forth who has an ownership interest in the business along with how much of an ownership interest the stockholder has. Normally, your principal stockholders section is broken down to include

the following: (a) each individual stockholder that owns more than 5% of the stock, (b) board members and (c) executive officers. For each person listed, the table should reflect the number of shares owned and the percentage such shares represent.

7. **Projected Financial Statements** – You have to be very careful with this section. On the one hand, you have this business model that you are putting your body and soul into. As far as you're concerned, it's the best business model ever and it's going to make a ton of money. While that level of enthusiasm and commitment is fully understandable and, if fact, I would be a bit concerned if I didn't see it in a new business owner, it must, at the same time, be tempered as it relates to the projected financial statements. Why? First, if the projected financial statements are not realistic, then you run the risk of losing some credibility. Finally, while most people understand and somewhat expect to see inflated projected financial statements, you want to properly manager everyone's expectations. So, when it comes to projected financial statements, I believe that it's better to be a bit more on the conservative side and either meet or exceed projections than the other way around. In terms of what should be included in your projected financial statements, it's recommended that you include the following at a minimum covering a 3-5 year period: (a) balance sheet, (b) income

statement and (c) assumptions. Your balance sheet reflects asset, liabilities and stockholder's equity at a point in time. The income statement reflects the projected revenue, the projected cost and a projection of whether there will be either net income or net loss for the year. It is not unusual to see a projected net loss for the first year or two depending upon the industry. So, once again, it's good to be as realistic as possible. The assumptions are critical as this will show that you've done your homework and the projected financial information does not entail numbers that have been pulled out of thin air.

Management Team

As you've probably figured out, I believe that the proper selection of a management team is critical. As I mentioned above, potential investors place a significant amount of weight on this component. The potential investors know that, as a general matter, investments in start-ups are very risky. So, when analyzing whether to make an investment in a start-up, potential investors are looking at several key components to make a judgment as to whether, all things being equal, a company is in the best possible position it can be in to succeed. As a result, this is one of those components you have to get right.

I know this sounds easy enough, but I also know what's probably going through your mind right now – how do you hire a solid management team without any money. Well, this is the threshold issue that most companies face when trying to bring on top manage-ment. So, let's begin with the basic question of what type of management team you should be looking to bring on board.

When making decisions about your management team, your first order of business, of course, should be trying to determine who would be the best person for the job. In conjunction with this, you also have to analyze it from the perspective of the investment com-munity. I bring this up because there may be certain attributes about one candidate that gives that person more credibility in the eyes of an investor. For exam-ple, let's assume that there are two very well qualified candidates for the position of chief financial officer. One candidate is a partner with a national accounting firm. The other candidate is a partner with a regional accounting firm but has also been the chief financial officer of a company that went through several rounds of financing and was recently sold. Which person do you think a potential investor will feel most comfortable with?

The next thing I want to point out, noting once again the importance of analyzing this issue with the invest-ment community in mind, is perhaps the most difficult thing most entrepreneurs have to deal with. This is the notion that although this new company may be your concept, and you have done all of the work thus far to get it off of the ground, it may be that you are not the best person to run the company. In other words, it may be in the long-term best interest of your company to have someone else come in as chief executive officer or president. I know this may sound strange but please allow me to explain. I have seen countless situations where the founder was absolutely brilliant and had developed and incredible concept or the founder was an incredible marketing person. However, that person had no experience running a business or possessed weak management skills. Trust me when I say that the investment community picks up on this point quickly, and they make judgments based upon this critical factor. In fact, I've seen situations where investors are interested in a company but will only invest if the founder(s) agree to bring in a new chief executive officer once the investment is made. There are many ways to make this work such that the founder maintains significant authority while not leading the company. For example, a new chief executive officer can be brought in while the founder is the president. This gives the founder the ability to learn on the job while the company is headed by a seasoned manager.

Finally, I want to address the issue of how a company can bring in such a strong management team when it has little or no initial capital. In this regard, there are a number of steps that can be taken. First, the company can set up an option program (as described below) and issue options as incentives. Second, the founders of the company can agree with investors that if initial funding is raised, part of the proceeds will be used to bring in new management. Third, the company can enter into strong employment agreements with individuals to further incentivize them to come on board. Also, if the founder hasn't done so already, that person initially may have to self-finance the company to put it in the best position possible.

At the end of the day, founders have to be objective about what skills they bring to the table. One thing about the investment community is that they do not beat around the bush. If they are not interested in the deal, they will let you know in no uncertain terms. So, if you're not sure whether your management team is either an asset or a liability, the investment community will gladly tell you.

Choice of Entity

Selecting the right choice of entity is another critical decision that has to be made. While there are several different types of entities that can be formed, we are only going to concentrate on two here: the corporation (both C and S) and the limited liability company. The reason I am only going to concentrate on these two types of entities is because, as a practical matter, your company will end up being one or the other. Additionally, I want to add at the outset that this is definitely an issue you should discuss with your attorney and/or your accountant before making a decision.

As I mentioned above, I'm only going to concentrate on the corporation (C and S) and the limited liability company. Although the S corporation and the limited liability company are derivatives of the tax code, even your analysis of whether to select a C corporation will be based largely upon the tax implications. I'll explain.

C Corporation

The C corporation is the entity most people are familiar with and the entity investors, as a general matter, are most comfortable with. In the C corporation context, the structure is such that it is generally authorized to issue stock. At a minimum, the entity will be authorized to issue common stock but if it is anticipated that the corporation will be raising capital, then it should be authorized to issued preferred stock as well. The differences between the two are the rights that attach to each. As a general matter, the sole right that attaches to common stock is the right to vote. For example, each share of common stock will constitute one vote. As to preferred stock, there are generally a bundle of rights that can attach to it. For example, in addition to voting rights, preferred stock can also have liquidation preferences, conversion rights and redemption rights just to name a few. What these terms mean exactly will be discussed in later chapters. In light of the fact preferred stock generally includes a bundle of rights, these are the shares that investors will normally want to purchase. Therefore, you will normally see your founders owning common stock, and the investors owning preferred stock.

In analyzing whether a C corporation is the best entity for you, there are a few things that should be considered. The primary advantages of a corporation include the following:

- Most investors are familiar with the C corporation structure and are comfortable with it.

- As a general matter, if your goal is to become a public company, then if you're not a C corporation already, you will ultimately have to convert to one.

- Case law for C corporations in most states is pretty well settled; therefore, there is very little doubt in terms of what is required by a corporation as well as the rights, privileges and responsibilities of its directors, officer and shareholders.

The primary disadvantage of a C corporation is tax related. Mechanically, when a C corporation generates revenue, it goes into the corporation. From there, the revenue can be used to pay expenses, salaries, dividends or reinvested into the corporation. From a tax perspective, when revenue goes into a corporation, the corporation has to pay taxes on it. Then, when the remaining revenue goes to employees in the form of salaries or to investors in the form of dividends, then they have to pay taxes on that income as well. Therefore, revenue that a C corporation generates is taxed twice, which is why you hear people say that C corporations are subject to "double taxation."

S Corporations

The S corporation, as I mentioned above, is derived from the tax code and is referred to as a flow-through entity. The reason an S corporation is referred to as a flow through entity is because, unlike a C corporation, revenue it generates goes straight through the corporation and up to the owners. The corporation, itself, pays no taxes on the revenue that is generated. That is the good news. The bad news is that in order to maintain its S corporation status under the tax code, the company must meet certain requirements. For example, it can only have one class of stock. Therefore, most S corporations are only authorized to issue common stock. Also, there is a limitation on the number of stockholders that can own an S corporation. This presents certain issues.

Namely, if you intend to raise capital, an S corporation is likely not the best entity for you because, as I mentioned above, investors, as a general matter, expect to receive preferred stock as consideration for their investments. Therefore, if you issue preferred stock (assuming you have already issued common stock to your founders), you will likely blow your S corporation status and will be treated by the Internal Revenue Service ("IRS") as a C corporation. As a result, while the S corporation is attractive because there is no double taxation, it may not be the best entity for you if the goal is to raise capital.

Limited Liability Company

Like the S corporation, the limited liability company ("LLC") is a flow-through entity. However, unlike the S corporations, the LLC does not have the same sort of restrictions. Therefore, as a general matter, the opportunities to raise capital under an LLC are available to you. So, on the positive side, there is no double taxation as it relates to an LLC. However, there are still a few issues you need to consider. First, the nomenclature is a bit different. Instead of stockholders, you have "members" in an LLC. Instead of a board of directors, an LLC has a board of managers. Also, as a general matter, an LLC issues "membership interests" or "units" as opposed to stock (although in some jurisdictions, you can form a "corporate style" LLC). Therefore, when it comes to raising capital, there may be some investors who are not as comfortable investing in an LLC. Also, there is not as much case law available for guidance with respect to LLCs as there is in relation to corporations.

MBE Considerations

In making these critical decisions, it is important that you continue to keep in mind the issue of whether you intend to seek MBE certification. Therefore, you want to make certain that your company does not fall outside of the parameters required in order to be an MBE at the outset. For example, what are the implications if a majority of the stock is owned by minorities but the chief executive officer is not a minority. What are the implications if a majority company owns a minority interest in the company? These are some of the real-life scenarios that exist and have to be thought through carefully as you organize your company.

CHAPTER 4

Angel Financing (Seed Capital)

The first stage in the financing life cycle is the angel or seed round. This is the round of financing where companies attempt to raise enough capital to get a solid infrastructure in place. This generally means that the corporation is attempting to raise capital to retain management and employees, purchase necessary assets and other general corporate matters. Normally, an "angel round" of financing can be as low as $250,000 and as high as $2,000,000. To truly understand this round of financing, however, we should begin by describing an "angel" investor.

Who are angel investors?

Angel investors can generally be broken up into two groups: (1) individual investors and (2) organized angel investor groups. Individual angel investors tend to be high net worth individuals that meet the accredited investor standard under the federal securities laws (I will explain the importance of this later), who are looking for investment opportunities that can potentially yield high rates of return. These investors generally have little to no involvement with respect to the operations of their portfolio companies. Normally, these are individuals that were entrepreneurs themselves and made large sums of money as a result of a successful liquidity event for their companies. They tend to have a significant amount of knowledge and expertise in certain areas and seek out new opportunities in those areas. You also tend to see a fairly large number of senior executives with large companies, entertainers and professional athletes entering the arena in an effort to invest their money in short-term, high risk/high return investments.

In an effort to gain access to a larger pool of potential deals to invest in, many angels are joining the more structured angel groups, which primarily operate in the following ways. There is one structure, whereby you have multiple angels that belong to a group. Generally, there is an individual (possibly someone that is not an angel) that is responsible for finding potential investment opportunities. Once an investment opportunity is found, then it is presented to the various angels in the group. The angels then vote on the opportunity as a group and if it is determined that it is something they want to invest in, then the angels, as a whole, make an investment. The second structure is similar to the first, except that rather than voting on the opportunity as a group, each angel can separately decide whether he or she is interested in investing. For example, there are ten angels in a group that have reviewed the offering documents for XYZ Corp. It may be that only three of the angels are interested in investing. If so, each angel would be responsible for negotiating his or her own deal. Neither deal is contingent upon the other. Some of these groups may be more structured than others. For example, some are set up as clubs that have monthly meetings, whereby certain companies are invited to make a presentation to the group's angels. In some instances, companies are asked to pay a fee to present. Needless, to say you should do your homework and perform your own due diligence before you approach these groups.

Where Can You Find Angels?

Although angels play a critical role in the financing life cycle, they are undoubtedly the hardest to find. Indeed, many angels do not publicize the fact that they are investors for fear of being bombarded by people who have no legitimate chance of receiving investment dollars. This goes back to the point I made earlier in the book about hiring a lawyer and possibly an accountant as early in the process as possible. This is so because most securities lawyers and accountants will have established relationships with angels and the investment community. This is important because, in many instances, angels will not give serious consideration to an investment opportunity, unless someone they know, and whose judgment they trust has referred the opportunity to them. In short, a large piece of the puzzle in terms of how you go about finding an angel goes back to relationships. Nevertheless, there are some steps you can take on your own to find potential angels, which include the following:

- **Internet** – The obvious place you can start is the internet. Interestingly, there are a couple of different things you will likely come across when searching for angel groups on the internet. First, you will see sites for some of these organized angel groups. It will likely set forth the criteria that the angels are looking for. For example, the angels may only be interested in companies that are in the technology space. There may also be geographic limitations. While most angels have no desire to have a significant say in the day to day operations of their portfolio companies, they tend to look for companies in their city or state such that they can have easy access to management if needed. Also, angels often help their portfolio companies by connecting them with other people they've established relationships with, so it is likely to be in the angel's best interest to keep everything local. Another set of sites you will see are those that are set up whereby everything is done over the internet for a fee. Normally, these sites will offer you the opportunity to submit a business plan and the operators of the site will attempt to match your plan with their stable of angels.

- **Placement Agent** – A placement agent is a qualified financial institution that specializes in finding investors for a deal. The placement agent can be one of the large investment banks or it can be a small firm that specializes in this type of work. Finding a good placement agent is something that your attorney and your accountant can help with as well. Utilizing a placement agent is obviously a more formal approach to the financing process. You will have to enter into a placement agent agreement with the firm, which will include a negotiated fee structure. Generally, the placement agent will ask for an up front fee, then you will also have to pay them a percentage of the funds that they locate.

- **Finders** – Finders are an informal version of the placement agents. Finders tend to be individuals who are well connected to high net worth individuals that are looking for investment opportunities (i.e., angels). Just like placement agents, some may ask for a small fee up front and will be paid a negotiated percentage of the funds they are able to bring in. However, there is normally a major difference between the finder and the placement agent, which can present a problem. If you noticed, when I described the placement agent, I referred to it as a "qualified financial institution." By this, I am saying (without getting into too much detail) that the placement agent is likely to be registered as a broker-dealer under the federal securities laws, which is required in order to properly perform this function. As a general matter, many of these finders are not registered broker-dealers, which could ultimately lead to problems for you. The reason this is so, goes back to the federal securities laws. In order for your company to issue securities, they either have to be registered with the Securities and Exchange Commission ("SEC") or they have to fall within an exemption. Normally, there are exemptions available to your company as it relates to the type of offering we're contemplating here (i.e., a private offering). However, if the finder is not a registered broker-dealer, then there is the possibility that you could ultimately lose your exemption, which would mean that your company has issued securities in violation of the federal securities laws. This is not something we want to have happen. In the past, finders appeared to have had a bit of wiggle room even if they were not registered broker-dealers. Some practitioners argued that finders did not violate federal securities laws if it only introduced a company to an investor that ultimately made an investment. Now, it appears as though there is little to no wiggle room as the SEC has made it clear that they are taking a strict stance on the issue. As a result, you have to be very careful and mindful of this issue when considering utilizing a finder.

- **Incubators** – Your standard incubator is an organized program, whereby, for a small fee, a select group of start-up entities are invited to utilize office space that will be made available to them and they will essentially be groomed to ultimately go off on their own. Normally, these incubators are non-profit entities that are available through universities, cities and other private organizations, who are attempting to facilitate economic development. These are outstanding programs that have relatively high levels of success. Often, these incubators will help you develop a business plan, introduce you to potential funding sources and help you create relationships that can be vital to your company's long-term success. There are also the for-profit incubators. These incubators are not as prolific as they once were during the hey-day of the technology boom but a few still appear to exist. Essentially, these had the same basic characteristics as the standard incubator structure; however, the entity operating the incubator would make an investment in each portfolio company. For example, XYZ Corp. would like to become one of Incubator X's portfolio companies. If Incubator X selected XYZ Corp. to enter the incubator, XYZ Corp. would have to sell a certain percentage of its stock (normally preferred stock) for $x cash. This would give XYZ Corp. the seed capital it needed to build its infrastructure, and it could take advantage of the services offered by Incubator X. In the meantime, Incubator X continues making these investments into each company that becomes a part of its program with the expectation that within 3-5 years each portfolio company will have an exit event that will allow it to generate a substantial return.

How to Protect Yourself

One of the concerns that entrepreneurs rightfully have when they are seeking financing is how to protect their ideas from being stolen. This is a reason-able question and the primary tool available to you is a nondisclosure agreement ("NDA"). Essentially, the NDA is an agreement restricting either one or both parties from disclosing information deemed confidential for a certain period of time. As a general matter, angel inves-tors, unlike venture capital firms, will agree to execute the NDA. You may get some resistance from those angels that are very active and feel they don't have enough time to read through each agreement. In these situations, you simply have a decision to make, which is whether the benefits of allowing a potential investor to read your material and possibly making an investment in your company outweigh the potential detriments associated with an investors not signing the NDA.

The Process of Raising Capital from Angels

To get to the point where you're actually prepared to begin raising capital, you hopefully have retained an attorney and possibly an accountant; you've finalized your business plan; you've formed your company and you have at least a skeleton management team in place. The next step is deciding how you want to approach the offering process. Essentially, you have two options.

Option one is what I call the global approach. If you take this approach, you will have an offering document prepared called a private placement memorandum ("PPM"). The general rule under the federal securities laws is that an issuer must either register securities being sold or the offering must fall under an applicable exemption. The exemptions most private offerings fall under require that certain information be disclosed to potential investors. Therefore, a PPM is drafted as it is an offering document that is provided to potential investors, pursuant to the federal securities laws, such that they can make informed investment decisions. Similar to a registration statement (discussed below), the PPM contains, among other things, information about the company, the securities being issued, risks associated with the offering, the company's capitalization and the biographies of management. In addition to the PPM, you also prepare a subscription agreement, which is the contract between the potential investor and the company. The potential investor will fill out the subscription agreement and indicate, among other things, how many shares of stock are being subscribed for and that it meets the definition of an accredited investor. The definition of what constitutes an accredited investor is set forth in the federal securities laws. As a general matter, accredited investors are individuals and institutions that based upon either income, net worth, size or experience have the financial wherewithal to withstand the loss of their entire investment. While the federal securities laws allow a company to sell securities to unaccredited investors, in certain limited circumstances, most securities lawyers counsel their clients to sell only to accredited investors such that they remain safely within the exemptions I referenced above. At the end of the day, this is an issue that should be discussed with your attorney.

Option two is where you expect to raise the entire capital from a single source. Therefore, the general approach is to negotiate a term sheet (some people refer to it as a letter of intent) with the party that is expected to make the investment. Once the term sheet is negotiated and executed, then the parties move forward to negotiate the definitive agreements – namely a stock purchase agreement and a shareholders' agreement.

Standard Terms

As was noted earlier, while it is not inappropriate to try an issue common stock, the more sophisticated investors will likely expect to receive preferred stock in exchange for their investment. Why, because as previously noted, preferred stock generally includes a bundle of rights that do not normally attach to common stock. A more detailed discussion of the types of terms of you can expect to negotiate can be found in the next chapter "Venture Capital."

How long should it take to obtain Angel financing?

The saying "timing is everything" is no less applicable to the funding process. In order to properly plan for the development of your business, you need to have a good understanding of how long the offering process generally takes. Everything, from a planning perspective, must be in sync as there may be contracts involved or limited opportunities available to you that are contingent on a successful raise of capital. In order to fully analyze the timing issue, I will break it up to cover the two options discussed above.

Option one: a global offering using a private placement memorandum that is disseminated to multiple potential investors. Under this option, there are two components to the timing issue. The first is how long it will take to fully prepare the offering documents and the last is how long can the offering generally stay open.

Assuming that the company has been properly formed, a business plan/executive summary has been prepared and financial statements are complete, then we can look solely at how long it will take to prepare offering documents. If not, then this could impact the timing in a substantial way by increasing the amount of time it will take to prepare the documents. We will assume, however, that the items referenced above have been properly prepared. If this is the case, then it is reasonable to expect an attorney to have a final version of the private placement memorandum and all appropriate ancillary documents ready for distribution in 2-4 weeks. Of course, there may be external factors that influence the preparation of these documents, which could obviously impact timing. However, this is a reasonable starting point, which should be confirmed with your attorney.

The next issue is how long can your company raise capital under the private placement memorandum. For example, let's assume that your company is attempting to raise $1,000,000. Can you use the offering document ad infinitum until you raise the entire $1,000,000 or is there some time limitation? While there is no hard line rule that answers this question per se, the generally accepted standard is six to seven months. Remember, the reason the company is disseminating the private placement memorandum to perspective investors is such that they can review the material and make an informed decision as to whether they want to make an investment. As a general matter, it's reasonable to assume that the information presented in the private placement memorandum will not become stale within that six to seven month period. On the other hand, the longer the company relies upon the private placement memorandum beyond that six or seventh month period, the greater the probability that there is something in the document that is no longer accurate or has become stale. If that is the case, then you begin to run the risk of being in violation of the securities laws for having false, misleading or omitted information in the document. Further, if an investor makes a decision to invest based upon information contained in the document that was either false, misleading or if material information is omitted, then the investor may have a basis for bringing an action against the company for violating the securities laws. Along these lines, if there is information relating to the company that develops while the offering is outstanding, then a determination has to be made as to whether it is material enough to warrant making a change to the private placement memorandum and sharing such information with those that have invested as well as those reviewing the offering document.

Min/Max Offering

In terms of analyzing the structure of your offering, one thing to keep in mind is whether you want to pursue what's referred to as a min/max offering (i.e., minimum/maximum offering). A min/max offering is one where it is determined that your company needs to raise X amount of dollars at a minimum, but the company wants X + Y dollars in order for the company to have an adequate amount of working capital. For example, you have started a technology company and the most pressing thing before you is the need to develop a prototype of your product. At the same time, you also want to hire management and acquire a manufacturing facility to produce your product. To develop the prototype, let's assume that it will cost $100,000 and to purchase the building and hire management, it will cost and additional $900,000. In this situation, you may elect to conduct a min/max offering of $100,000 minimum and a maximum of $1,000,000.

The reason you may elect to take this approach is because you know that unless you raise the $100,000 to build the prototype, then you can't move forward with your business model. So, if you raise only $40,000, then none of the objectives can be achieved. Investors will be aware of this as well; therefore, they will be concerned about investing in your company, if you do not raise the $100,000 to build the prototype. This likely means that it will be difficult, if not impossible to repay their investment amount let alone generating a return. This is why the min/max offering approach can be attractive in some circumstances because, under this structure, you will return all of the money you have raised if you do not raise the minimum $100,000. This way the investor is not harmed, and you can evaluate the situation and determine how to move forward.

Valuation

I must say that one thing that absolutely drives me insane is when a client retains me to help with the offering process and it has already conveyed to someone or to potential investors how much stock it is going to sell, at what price and what the return will be without taking into account the valuation issue. This not only shows that the issuer has not done its homework but it shows a lack of sophistication, which should raise a red flag in any investor's mind. An entire book can be written about this issue alone, but my recommendation is that you keep in mind the following:

- Unless you have thought through the valuation issue and have a reasonable basis for your valuation, I recommend that you neither discuss nor put in writing (e.g., in your business plan) anything regarding the number of shares you plan to offer or the offering price until this has been discussed with your attorney and/or a third party that can provide an independent valuation analysis. In those situations where you have a board or an individual on the board that is sophisticated as it relates to these sorts of financial matters, then the conclusion of the board should suffice. While there are varying opinions as to whether you ever put in writing what the return on investment will be, I have always recommended against it.

- If you are either a start-up entity or in the early stages of development, it may be prudent to plan stages of financing, rather than going for the homerun, such that you do not have to sell more of the company than needed. For example, you may decide that the company absolutely needs $250,000 as soon as possible in order to be sustainable. However, the best-case scenario is to raise $2,000,000 in order to put all of the things the company needs into place. In this situation, it may be prudent to simply go after the $250,000 first, if your company has a modest valuation at this time, and raise an additional amount down the road once the company's value has increased.

A more detailed analysis of the valuation issue will be discussed under the chapter entitled "Venture Capital."

Alternative Sources of Seed and Early Stage Financing

Being resourceful is half the battle when it comes to a start-up company. For the most part, you have to stretch your resources, and your efforts should always be directed towards maximizing opportunities. Therefore, it is always helpful to know of legitimate opportunities that are available to you. In this regard, there are three alternative sources of seed and early stage capital that you should be aware of.

Business Consortium Fund

The Business Consortium Fund ("BCF") is the financing arm of the NMSDC. It is a critical component of NMSDC's overall mission of providing a nexus between MBEs and corporate America. Based in New York, the BCF is a non-profit entity that provides financing and business support to MBEs. BCF provides financing and business services through its network of strategic alliance partners to MBEs that need capital and business support services to grow their businesses but have been unable to raise capital through conventional sources. BCF has the capacity to either make loans or to take on an equity position. Specifically, investments by BCF can be made in one of three ways:

1. Subordinated debt paid over a minimum period of five (5) years.

2. Subordinated debt, paid over a minimum period of five (5) years, with an equity feature allowing BCF's affiliated entity to acquire a percentage of the company through the exercise of warrants.

3. A straight equity investment in a company.

In order for an MBE to be eligible for consideration of a loan, the following criteria must be met:

1. The business must be certified by the NMSDC.

2. The loan must be for business purposes.

3. The business must have contracts/purchase orders with or a meaningful supplier relationship with a NMSDC corporate member or a corporate member of a NMSDC affiliated Regional Purchasing Council.

In order for an MBE to be considered for an equity investment, the following criteria must be met:

1. The business must be certified by the NMSDC.

2. The business must meet the Small Business Administration's ("SBA") definition of a "Small Business" that is eligible for investment by a Specialized Small Business Investment Company (i.e., net worth less than $18 million and

average net income for the last two years of less than $6 million).

3. The business must have a business relationship with a corporate member of the NMSDC or one or more of its affiliated Regional Councils.

You can learn more about BCF by going to its website at www.bcfcapital.com.

Small Business Innovative Research Programs

I first learned of the Small Business Innovative Research ("SBIR") program while attending a venture capital conference in Washington, DC several years ago. Not only was I surprised to find out that such a program existed, but I was also pleasantly surprised to hear that many of these programs were attempting to encourage MBEs to consider them as financing alternatives.

The SBIR program, along with its sister program, the Small Business Technology Transfer ("STTR") is administered by the SBA. The goal of the programs is to ensure that small, high-tech innovative businesses are significant parts of the federal government's research and development efforts that have the potential for commercialization. The main difference between the SBIR and the STTR programs is that the STTR program requires that the business entity formally collaborate with a research institution.

As a general matter, the program is structured such that a business can respond to a solicitation, by a governmental agency, for funding. This generally requires that the business provide a business plan and other ancillary information. If the agency determines that the technology is something that may be of interest, then the business is invited to present to a panel. The NSF, for example, creates a panel consisting of other business owners such that there is a diverse set of opinions from experts that are knowledgeable about various areas of technology. Once the presentation is made, the panel will provide its recommendation to NSF, who will then make a decision as to whether the business should be awarded a grant. If the business is awarded a grant, then it may be eligible to receive another grant after a certain period of time, if it is determined that there is some commercial viability to the technology.

The amount of the award granted varies among the various agencies. Additionally, the amount of time it may take from the moment a business responds to a solicitation to the time it is awarded a grant may vary as well. There are some agencies where a business can be awarded as much as $500,000 per grant. Also, there are some agencies where it takes as little as six months to be awarded a grant. So, in the grand scheme of things this is fairly significant seed money and the amount of time it might take to be awarded a grant may not be much greater than what you could expect to encounter through the equity process. The key thing to note about the SBIR/STTR programs is that they primarily seek technology companies for potential funding.

State Seed Programs

As quiet as it's kept, there are several state sponsored seed programs that are designed to diversify the state's economy by funding innovative companies in industries the states seek to promote. By and large, these programs are equity investments with terms not unlike what angels generally seek. These programs are structured in a variety of ways. For example, Georgia's seed program is called the ATDC Seed Capital Fund ("Seed Fund") and under this program, the Seed Fund collaborates with other investors such that it will invest $1 for every $3 of private investment. The Seed Fund can invest up to $1 million in any one company. As can be seen, this is a potentially fertile source of funding.

Microfinance

The microfinance industry is a growing industry that deserves some attention. Originally, the microfinance industry was originally structured to provide small amounts of financing to the poor in economically depressed countries. The idea is to fill in the gaps left by banks through providing loans and financial services to individuals who have little to no income. The common example is a $500 loan to someone in an economically depressed country to buy a sewing machine and other items to begin a sewing business. This model has proven to be generally successful and is now available not only in the poorer countries but in the U.S. as well but on a much larger scale.

Microfinance companies in the U.S. tend to make low interest loans to start-up companies that have received little to no capital from other sources. While the maximum loan amounts available through these microfinance entities are fairly small (generally between $4,000 - $10,000), it can make a huge difference in the very early stages of development.

CHAPTER 5

Venture Capital

Venture capital funds are professionally managed entities organized for the sole purpose of investing in potentially high growth companies with the expectation of generating high rates of return on their initial investments. This is a key component of the financing life cycle but it is one of the least understood. I've found that there are many misconceptions about the venture capital industry such as:

- I will never get a fair valuation from a venture capital firm.

- You have to be a large company in order to obtain venture capital.

- Venture capital firms will want to take over my company.

- All venture capital firms think about is the exit event.

- I will have to sell more than 51% of my company in order to obtain venture capital and this will cause me to lose my minority status.

I could go on but this gives you a good snapshot of some of the things I've heard over the years about the venture capital industry. So, before we can begin to analyze this aspect of the financing life cycle, I think we have to begin by explaining what a venture capital firm is and how it operates.

Formation of a Venture Capital Fund

As a general matter, the principals of a fund will form a general partnership first. Often, the general partnership will be structured as a corporation. The purpose of the general partnership is to serve as the actual manager of the day to day operations of the fund and it is the entity responsible for making the business decisions relating to the fund. Once the general partnership is formed, a limited partnership is created. Organizationally, a limited partnership agreement will be prepared that will outline the terms under which the limited partnership will operate; the general partner will own at least 1% of the limited partnership and the general partner will be entitled to carried interest (i.e., fees) from the limited partnership equal to 20% of the gains generated by the fund.

The next step is for the limited partnership to begin raising capital. Just like any entity that seeks to raise capital, the limited partnership must have a private placement memorandum prepared and all appropriate ancillary documents. The limited partnership, through its general partner, then begins the process of trying to raise capital. Generally, the limited partnership will reach out to pension funds and other institutional investors in order to raise the capital. As the limited partnership is a flow-through entity (as discussed above), the limited partners will make money only if there is some event where the limited partnership makes money. This is why the "exit" or "liquidity" event is so important to the fund because, as a general matter, only if a portfolio company is sold or goes public will the limited partnership make money, which it can use, in turn, to pay its limited partners.

Based upon this background, the obvious should be clear, which is that (1) funds are under tremendous pressure to make investments in companies that have high growth potential; (2) it is in a fund's best interest to do everything it can to help put companies in its portfolio in the best position to succeed; (3) that a fund's returns should be high enough to incentivize limited partners to participate in future funds organized by the fund organizers and (4) funds feel the need to seek terms that give it the greatest amount of flexibility and leverage with respect to its portfolio companies. All of these points are important because if the returns are not adequate, then the fund may have difficulty raising capital for future funds.

When are you ready to begin seeking venture capital?

Hopefully with this background, you are better positioned to understand the business issues associated with raising funds from a venture capital fund's perspective. That being said, if you want to give your company the ammunition to put itself in the best position to grow, then you generally have to, at least, consider raising capital from a venture capital fund. Indeed, this coincides with my basic premise that MBEs must continue to be transformational in their approach towards business by concentrating in high growth industries and thinking globally. In fact, many venture funds will only concentrate on industries they believe have high growth potential.

The threshold question, however, is how do you know you're ready to begin seeking venture capital. At a minimum, the following factors should be considered:

- Just as with angel financing, you should have a detailed business plan in place that clearly sets forth the company's business model.

- By now, you should have had at least one round of financing in place, thereby allowing you to bring in a solid management team. If angels look hard at the management team, venture capital funds look even harder. When I call friends in the venture community about clients, the first question they always ask is how is the management team. This point can not be overstated.

- It certainly helps if someone either on the management team or on the board of directors has experience with a company that has successfully raised capital before. This gives the fund additional comfort that there is a seasoned team in place that knows the process and is capable of leading the company in the right direction.

- There should be someone on your team (e.g., lawyer, accountant or board member) that has ties to the venture capital community because, as noted above, venture funds generally will not take a serious look at a company unless it has been referred to them by someone whose judgment they trust.

- Is your financial house in order? One of the items a venture fund will seek as part of its due diligence is your financial information. Further, if the fund elects to invest in your company, it will seek to make sure that it receives your financial information on a periodic basis. So, please be prepared to provide the fund with a reliable set of financial statements.

- Have you done your homework? Research the venture capital firms you might be interested in before you approach it for capital. Many venture capital funds concentrate on certain industries. So, be sure to determine that your company is in an industry that the fund likes to invest in before you approach it in order to save some time and prevent potential embarrassment.

- Are you in a growth industry? This, of course, is something the fund will investigate in order to gauge whether your company is in an industry that has the potential to grow at a level that can allow it to generate the returns it seeks.

- How strong is your board of directors? Is the board experienced and has a diverse background. As I noted before, the fund is seeking as much comfort as possible. Therefore, anything you can do to give them the comfort they need to make the investment should be considered.

- In terms of the amount of funds being sought, you often hear that it is easier to get funding at $5 million and above as venture funds look to make larger investments. There is a certain level of truth to this. However, there are venture funds that invest at much smaller amounts and at earlier stages of a company's development. This highlights, once again, the importance of researching as much as you can about funds before approaching them.

Beyond the above, there are multiple variables a venture fund considers in analyzing its investment options. For example, the venture fund will also take into consideration your geographic location relative to its location. As a general matter, venture funds like to invest in geographic locations that are somewhat close to the funds base of operations. Also, the limited partnership agreement may place limitations on investments in certain geographic areas or they may encourage investments in others. Therefore, at the end of the day, you must do everything you can to have everything in order and be prepared to convey a story to the fund that captures its attention.

Selecting the right venture funds to pursue

On the one hand, a business may say to itself that cash is king and it doesn't matter which venture fund actually makes the investment. On the other hand, some businesses may say that they view an investment by a venture fund as a partnership; therefore, they should be as selective as the venture fund in determining whether to accept its capital. I suspect the truth is probably somewhere in the middle in that if a company didn't need capital it wouldn't be in the process of seeking capital from venture funds in the first place; therefore, it has to be realistic about its expectations. That being said, I think it is wise for a company to understand as much as possible about the various venture funds it's interested in before consummating any transaction. As such, the business should be proactive and seek to find out as much about a venture firm as possible such as the following:

- What industry or industries does the venture fund have the most experience?

- Is it likely that the venture fund will commit the time and energy needed to help your company grow?

- Do management and the venture fund have a shared vision with respect to the growth and development of your company?

- What is the quality, diversity and depth of a venture fund's resources (e.g., professionals, staff, consultants and industry contacts)?

- What is the chemistry between management and the venture firm's designated representatives?

- Is there a willingness on the part of the venture fund to help secure future rounds of capital if needed?

- What are the venture fund's views on the depth, coverage and adequacy of your management team and its ability to assist in recruiting and retaining critical management personnel?

Valuation

Assuming that the venture firm is interested in moving forward, the next question centers around valuation. In this regard, many venture firms refer to the "pre-money" and "post-money" valuation of a business. The "pre-money" valuation is the agreed upon value of the business before the venture fund's investment is made. The "post-money" valuation is the pre-money valuation plus the amount invested by the venture fund. For purposes of this analysis, we will work from the perspective of what percentage will the venture fund receive for its investment. Therefore, we will begin with the post-money valuation and work our way forward. For example, if the venture fund receives 1/3 of the company's equity based upon an investment of $2 million, then the post-money valuation would be $6 million (3 x $2 million) and the pre-money valuation would be $4 million ($6 million post-money minus the $2 million investment).

As part of its valuation analysis, the venture firm, as noted above, will conduct a thorough analysis of your company's financial statements. If there are only projections available then the venture fund may consider multiple factors because of the uncertainty associated with projections. For example, the venture firm may begin by looking at the standard valuation given to a company of similar size and experience in the industry. From there, the venture firm may look at other characteristics to make appropriate adjustments such as the experience of the management team and the board of directors. The venture fund may also consider whether it is anticipated that future rounds of financing will be needed. When multiple rounds of financing are involved, then the ownership interests of prior investors will be diluted. Therefore, if it is anticipated that future rounds will be needed, then the venture fund may seek a larger ownership interest in the beginning.

One of the measures discussed when an agreement can't be reached as to valuation is a performance-based adjustment approach (through options or warrants). This approach allows the venture fund to receive more stock in the company if certain pre-set financial bench marks are either met or not met.

Term Sheet

The term sheet provides a summary of the key aspects of the transaction that the parties agree upon before moving to the next stage of the proposed financing. Attorneys have different philosophies about the level of detail that should be included in a term sheet. In this regard, some try to minimize the level of detail included in term sheet in hopes that once the term sheet is executed, the momentum of the transaction will propel it forward even if there is a glitch in the process moving forward. At the same time, there are others who want the term sheet to be as detailed as possible to reduce the chances of there being any surprises. As a general matter, it is probably in everyone's best interest to have a reasonably detailed term sheet such that the parties have a reasonably clear understanding of the transaction's structural components.

A term sheet is not a contract and, generally, it is not binding on the parties. However, there may be instances where the parties desire the terms to be binding and thereby draft the term sheet as a binding agreement.

A sample term sheet for a first round of financing is set forth below:

Term Sheet
Series A Convertible Preferred Stock

Issuer:	XYZ, Corp. (the "Company")
Currently Outstanding Securities:	2,000,000 shares of fully-diluted Common Stock equivalents.[1]
Investor:	Venture Capital, LP ("VC").
Amount of Investment:	$1,000,000 for 1,000,000 shares of Series A Convertible Preferred Stock ("Series A").
Price Per Share:	$1.00 per share.
Minimum Investment	$100,000 per investor.

[1] To determine the number of "fully-diluted" shares outstanding, you must include issued stock plus shares that are subject to outstanding options, warrants and similar equity instruments including reserved shares.

Amount:

Minimum to Close: $500,000.

Closing: The Company and VC agree to use their best efforts to close the transaction on or about _____, 20__.

Conditions to Closing: An investment by VC is subject to the following conditions:

- satisfactory completion of due diligence;
- satisfactory review by VC of all relevant documents;
- negotiation and execution of definitive agreements; and
- other conditions customary to closing.

Description of Series A:

(1) Dividend Provisions: Holders of Series A will receive a 6% noncumulative dividend when, as and if declared by the Board of Directors. Dividends on shares of Common Stock will not be paid during any year until a 6% dividend has been paid on the Series A and no dividend in excess of $0.06 will be paid on shares of Common Stock.[2]

---

2   The noncumulative dividend feature means that holders of Series A receive dividends only if the Board determines that it is in the best interest of the company to pay such dividends. As a general matter,

(2) Liquidation Preference:

Upon either the liquidation, dissolution or winding up of the Company, holders of Series A will be entitled to receive in preference to the holders of Common Stock an amount equal to $1.00 per share, plus any declared but unpaid dividends ("Liquidation Amount").

After payment of the above preference, holders of Series A will share with holders of Common Stock all remaining proceeds available for distribution to shareholders on an "as converted to common" basis.[3]

(3) Redemption:

Commencing three years after closing (mandatory redemption date), at the request of holders of at least 600,000 shares of Series A, the Company will redeem all (but not less than all) the

companies tend to reinvest their capital; therefore, it is not uncommon for companies to refrain from paying dividends until they go public (if ever). On the other hand, cumulative dividends automatically accrue over time even if the company neither declares nor pays dividends.

3   This is commonly referred to as "participating" preferred stock, which grants holders not only a preference over the common stock equal to the original purchase price of the preferred stock plus accrued dividends, but also a right to share with the common shareholders assets that remain after payment of the preferences.

Series A held by such holders by paying in cash the Liquidation Amount for the shares being redeemed. All other Series A holders will be notified and provided with an opportunity for redemption. If the Company has insufficient funds legally available to fully discharge its redemption obligations, funds that become available thereafter will be applied to redeem the Series A until such obligation is fully discharged.

(4) Conversion: A holder of Series A will have the right to convert Series A, at the option of the holder, at any time, into shares of Common Stock. The number of shares of Common Stock into which each share of Series A may be converted initially will be determined by dividing $1.00 (initial price) by the conversion price. The initial conversion price of the Series A is $1.00 (conversion price).

(5) Automatic Conversion: The outstanding Series A will be automatically converted into Common Stock on the closing of an underwritten public offering of shares of common stock at a public offering price per share of at least $5.00 with aggregate proceeds of at least $15,000,000 and a post-offering market capitalization of at least $25,000,000 (a "Qualified Public Offering"). Such conversion will be at the applicable conversion price in effect on the day next preceding the closing of the Qualified Public Offering.

(6) Registration Rights: Holders of Series A will be entitled to two demand registrations at the expense of the Company and unlimited piggyback registration rights; provided, however, that no demand may be made prior to the second anniversary of the closing.

(7) Voting Rights: Except (i) with respect to the election of directors as described under "Board Representation" below, (ii) with respect to certain protective provisions as described under "Protective Provisions" below and (iii) as expressly provided herein, Series A holders will vote with the holders of Common Stock as a single class on all matters. Series A holders will have the right to that number of full shares of Common Stock issuable upon conversion of the Series A.

(8) Protective Provision: Without the consent of the holders of at least a majority of the Series A (voting as a single class), the Company shall not, and will not permit any subsidiary to, (i) create or issue any equity security senior to or on a parity with the Series A as to dividend, liquidation or redemption rights; (ii) sell all or substantially all the assets of the Company or any subsidiary or consolidate or merge the Company or any subsidiary; (iii) amend the Articles of Incorporation or Bylaws of the Company or (iv) take certain other actions materially affecting the Series A.

Information Rights: As long as any Series A is outstanding, the Company will deliver to each holder of Series A annual and quarterly financial statements and other information reasonably requested by a holder of the Series A. Holders of Series A will also be entitled to advise the Company as to its management and to discuss its affairs with key employees.[4]

Use of Proceeds: Proceeds from the sale of Series A will be used for general working capital purposes.

Board Representation: The Articles of Incorporation and the Bylaws will provide that the authorized number of Directors will be seven. Pursuant to the Articles of Incorporation, the Series A (voting as a class) will have the right to elect three directors.

Shareholders' Agreement: All existing shareholders (Common and Series A) will execute a Shareholders' Agreement with the Company pursuant to which the

---

4   Venture capital firms often seek fairly extensive information and reporting provisions such as monthly financials, annual budgets and forecasts and management reports.

Company and the holders of Series A and Common Stock have a right of first refusal with respect to any shares proposed to be sold by any shareholder. The Investors will also receive co-sale rights on any proposed sale of shares by an existing shareholder. The Shareholders Agreement will also give the Company and the holders of Common Stock and Series A the right to repurchase certain of the shares of a management member in the event his employment with the Company terminates. The number of shares and the price per share will depend on the reason for termination. Each of the Investors will be entitled to purchase its pro rata share of any proposed new issuance of equity securities by the Company. The Shareholders Agreement will terminate upon a Qualified Public Offering, certain mergers or a sale of substantially all the Company's assets.

Employment Agreements: _____ and _____ (key employees) will each enter into an employment and noncompetition agreement with the Company in connection with the Series A financing.

Purchase Agreement: The purchase of the Series A will be made pursuant to a Preferred Stock Purchase Agreement ("Purchase Agreement"). Such Agreement will contain, among other things, appropriate representations and warranties of the Company and the VC, covenants of the Company and the VC reflecting the provisions set forth herein and other restrictive negative and affirmative covenants customary for transactions of this type and appropriate additional conditions of closing. Until the Purchase Agreement is signed by both the Company and the VC, no binding obligation will exist on the part of any party to consummate the transaction.

Expenses: The Company will reimburse VC for the reasonable legal expenses of a single counsel not to exceed $_____, incurred with respect to the transactions described herein.

A general description of some of the key concepts included in the term sheet are set forth below:

Board Representation – Venture capital funds, as a general matter, seek representation on the boards of their portfolio companies. The number of seats a venture fund has on the board is usually a function of the size of its investment. This is a negotiated point that both parties generally seek to find middle ground on. Understandably, the venture fund desires to have representation on the board in an effort to provide some level of input and, in some cases, some level of control in an effort to protect its investment. The company, on the other hand, while understanding that the venture fund will likely want some representation on the board, will generally resist giving up too many seats on the board in hopes of maintaining some level of control.

Equity Incentives – In an effort to further incentivize employees, directors and other designated individuals to help make the company a success, even if they are not receiving substantial sums of money, the company may issue equity incentives, in the form of options generally, to these individuals. To do so, the company must create a Stock Incentive Plan ("SIP") that creates the framework under which the company can issue equity incentives. Beyond, stock options, the company can issue other types of equity incentives under the SIP such as restricted stock awards. However, you generally see stock options as the primary tool companies use as an equity incentive. Stock options are derivatives of the tax code; therefore, a company must be very careful about how they are structured, who they're issued to and the circumstances under which they are issued. There are two types of options: (i) Incentive Stock Options ("ISO") and (ii) Non-Qualified Stock Options ("NSO"). Stock options are securities that give a grantee the right to exercise the options over a period of time and purchase a certain number of shares in the company at what is hoped to be a discounted price (the "Exercise Price"). For example, Company XYZ issues to Employee A an option to purchase 100 shares of common stock over a four (4) year period. Rights to purchase shares under the option vest evenly over the four (4) year period at 25% each year. In other words, at the end of year 1, Employee A is eligible to purchase 25% or 25 shares at the Exercise Price. With respect to the Exercise Price, it must be the value of the stock on the date of grant. Thus, if the value of the stock on the date of grant is $1.00 per share, then the Exercise Price for the stock should be $1.00. The idea is that the value of the company will continue to grow, thereby, the value of the stock will continue to increase. So, if Employee A exercises his or her options and the value of the stock continues to increase, then Employee A will not only have an ownership interest in the company but will hopefully be able to sell the stock in the future at a profit. To further illustrate using our example set forth above, where Employee A receives an option to purchase 100 shares with an Exercise Price of $1.00 per share and 25% of the options vest each year for four years, Employee A might elect to exercise the options at the end of year four (4). Let's assume that Company XYZ's value has increased substantially over the four year period and, now, the price per share is $10 per share. Rather than Employee A paying $1,000 to purchase the 100 shares (i.e., 100 shares at $10 per share), Employee A exercises the option to purchase all 100 shares at the Exercise Price (i.e., $1.00); therefore, he or she only pays $100 to purchase 100 shares that have a fair market value of $1,000. As you can see, this is a powerful tool in the company's arsenal that helps incentivize people to make the company as successful as possible.

Redemption – The primary issue a venture capital firm is concerned about is whether it can get a return on its investments. For that venture fund to make a return on the investment, some event must take place where its return can be materialized. This is referred to as a "liquidity" or "exit" event, which will be discussed in detail in the next chapter. In addition to the liquidity or exit event, venture firms seek to have a redemption feature added to the purchase agreement knowing that it wants to be out of an investment within 5 to 7 years after making the initial investment. As a general matter, the redemption provision provides that under certain circumstances, the company will purchase all of the stock held by the venture firm at a specific price. Mechanically, the redemption provision might give the venture firm the right to require the company to redeem, or buy back, the venture firm's stock after a certain period of time at a preset price. Alternatively, the redemption provision could give the company the right, at its option, to purchase back its stock from the venture firm after a certain period of time at a preset price. Under either circumstance, the redemption price will usually have a built in return for the investor.

Registration Rights – As noted above, the venture firm is trying to position itself to make a return on its investment and this normally materializes at the time a liquidity or exit event occurs. One such event is an initial public offering, which will be discussed below. In this situation, the venture firm wants to be in position to sell its stock in the open market. To do so, a couple of things must first occur. First, the venture firm, who presumably has convertible preferred stock, must be able to convert such stock into common stock as this is what will need to be sold in the open market. Finally, such shares must be registered with the Securities and Exchange Commission in order for the company to comply with the federal securities laws. Therefore, in order to be in position to have these things occur, the venture firm will seek to have a contractual right, through the purchase agreement, to have "piggyback" and "demand" registration rights. Piggyback registration rights give the venture firm the right to register certain of its common shares for sale with state and federal authorities when the company or founding shareholders decide to register their own common shares. Demand registration rights give the venture firm the right to force a company to register their shares upon its request.

Co-Sale Rights – Before reaching a liquidity or exit event, founders and other key shareholders may receive offers from third parties to purchase their shares. Oftentimes, such sales are structured in order for the founders and/or key shareholder to receive premiums on their shares. If such an event were to occur, the venture firm could find itself in the position as a minority shareholder in a non-public business without any viable route to liquidity. Accordingly, the venture firm will seek to have "co-sale" rights, which allow the venture firm to participate in a sale of common stock by selling shares alongside other shareholders, who have received an offer to purchase their shares from a third party, on a proportional basis.

Founder Employment Agreements – Founders and/or early investors who may also be managers understandably are cognizant of the impact an investment by a venture fund will have on their ability to influence the direction of the company. Indeed, founders and certain key employees are critical to the company's success and the loss of such individuals can have an adverse impact on its operations. Therefore, while key individuals may desire to have employment agreements in place, venture firms may not be as desirous as they may want flexibility with respect to management.

What to expect once a Venture Fund Makes an Investment

Before an investment transaction is consummated, the company and the venture firm will discuss the ultimate objectives of both parties including use of proceeds, timelines for achieving certain milestones, internal and external growth expectations and the ultimate liquidity event. The venture firm's role will be to help impose discipline on the process and will seek regular and timely information about the company. Further, the venture firm will seek a reporting and budgeting process and monitor to evaluate the growth of both business and management to determine whether they have developed in accordance with the plan. The venture firm will also pay close attention to governance policies and procedures.

The company should be less concerned about whether it will maintain its control over the day-to-day operations of the company as this is normally not a desire of the venture firm. Moreover, it generally is not practical for a venture firm to attempt to exert control over the day-to-day activities of its portfolio companies. Instead, venture firms generally insist on being kept abreast of the big-picture issues.

Finally, a venture firm will likely want to ensure that the company stays on course with the previously discussed game plan and will want to be advised if there are any deviations. The venture firm will also expect to have a voice in, if not some level of control (or veto rights) over, the company's pursuit of additional financing and exit strategies. In this regard, a venture firm will seek to provide guidance and influence with respect to the exit strategy or liquidity event that is the best mechanism to ultimately yield the highest rate of return.

Impact on MBE Status

One of the common issues that minority-owned companies in general and certified minority-owned companies in particular are always cognizant of is the impact a capital raise will have on the company's ability to maintain minority ownership of at least 51% of the stock. This is particularly critical for certified minority-owned companies as the NMSDC's certification process is based on 51% ownership, operation and control by minority individuals. Therefore, certified minority-owned companies rightfully had trepidations about trying to raise capital from venture firms for fear that they would lose their 51% control and, thereby, potentially lose their certification.

In an effort to address these issues, the NMSDC put into place a measure referred to as the "Growth Initiative" that seeks to act as a framework under which MBEs can grow and access capital while retaining management and control. Under the initiative, NMSDC's certification process remains the same and it only affects those NMSDC-certified companies that seek equity capital from professional institutional investors through the issuance of a new class of non-voting stock. Exceptions to the 51% ownership requirement will be made by the NMSDC on a case-by-case basis. In these situations, a minority business may be certified by the NMSDC if the minority owners own at least 30% of the company's economic equity, which occurs when non-minority investors purchase a majority of its equity. Therefore, in these situations, a business may be certified if the following criteria are met:

i.   Minority management/owners control the day-to-day operations of the company.

ii. Minority management/owners retain a major-
     ity (no less than 51%) of the company's voting
     equity.

iii. Minority owner/s operationally control the
     board of directors (i.e., must appoint a majority
     of the board of directors).

Finally, in order to certify under this framework, the
MBE's non-minority investor must be a "professional
institutional investor" that is approved by the NMSDC's
certifying committee. NMSDC defines "professional
institutional investor" as a firm that (a) is in the business of making equity investments (not managing
businesses) and (b) manages more than $25 million in
capital.

State Venture Funds

As a means of creating more jobs and economic
development, states have been allocating to their own
venture programs that invest directly into companies
and/or invest into fund of funds. A fund of funds is a
venture firm that raises capital to make investments in
other venture firms as oppose to a portfolio of companies. In those instances where a state creates and invests
in a fund of funds, that fund will normally make investments in venture funds, either inside or outside of that
state, that has a history of investing in companies in that
state. Depending upon the fund, these state run funds
make investments in everything from the seed round
to later stages of investment. The state run funds are
fertile ground for potential sources of financing as they
often make investments at levels that a typical venture

fund may resist. Further, as noted above, many venture firms are fairly conservative in terms of the geographic locations they invest in, because, among other things, they want to have quick and easy access to management. Moreover, the venture firms may feel that a certain state does not have enough deal flow to warrant any particular attention. In these situations, state run venture programs are an attractive alternative as they are looking for investment opportunities in their specific states in an effort to create economic opportunity.

CHAPTER 6

Exit or Liquidity Event

Many people tend to believe that this final phase of the financing life cycle, known as the exit or liquidity event, is the most important. However, I can't say that I fully endorse this belief. Why – because if there is a misstep along the way, it can come back to haunt you in this final phase. For example, I once handled an initial public offering, and our client was sailing through the registration process. As discussed below, during the course of the registration process, you have to address any issues raised by the Securities and Exchange Commission ("SEC"). Well, we receive a comment letter from the SEC and one of the questions related to the companies' stock options and how they were priced. Prior to its initial public offering ("IPO"), we had not been the client's outside counsel. Therefore, we performed detailed due diligence with respect to this new client and, during the course of our due diligence, we noticed that the exercise price on the company's options seemed a bit low. When we discussed it with the client, they were able to satisfy us that the exercise prices on the options were appropriate. Had we been counsel from the beginning, however, we likely would have advised the client to take a different approach. So, while we weren't necessarily surprised by the SEC's inquiry, we knew where they were headed. The SEC's inquiry about the stock options was significant, because they were trying to determine whether the client had issued what's referred to as "cheap stock," which is the issuance of options with artificially low exercise prices before an IPO. If it's determined that, in fact, cheap stock was issued, it can present fairly significant issues. Initially, the SEC was not satisfied with our response, but we eventually worked through the issue, and the company went public. The point here is that if you don't have everything done correctly on the front end, it may harm your chances of having a successful exit or liquidity event on the back end.

The exit or liquidity event (the words are used interchangeably), is a transaction that gives those who have an ownership interest in the company an opportunity to generate a return on the investment. If you're an investor, this is the transaction you have been waiting for as it will present you with an opportunity to hopefully recoup your original investment plus more so that you can have a return on the investment. The primary exit events available to a company include: initial public offerings, sale of the company, management buyouts and stock redemptions. The two most prevalent exit events are the initial public offering and the sale of the company, which are discussed below.

Initial Public Offerings

In 1990, I started working for the SEC in the Division of Corporation Finance ("Corporation Finance"), which is the transactional arm of the agency. The SEC has some of the smartest and hardest working individuals I've ever met. This should be comforting news to most people as the SEC is at the epic center of our capital markets. In this regard, all companies that seek to go public must file their registration statements with the SEC and, within the agency, it is the Corporation Finance's staff that handles these transactions. So, as a staff attorney in Corporation Finance, I handled countless IPOs and it didn't take me long to realize a couple of things. First, an IPO is an incredible mechanism to not only grow a company but a mechanism to create an incredible amount of personal wealth. Finally, with this being the case, I was absolutely shocked at how few minority-owned companies, particularly companies owned by African-Americans, there were whose shares were publicly traded. In fact, when I started in 1990, although I'm sure there must a been a few, I'm unaware of any African-American owned company whose stock was traded on either the New York Stock Exchange ("NYSE") or Nasdaq. In fact, it wasn't until 1991, when Black Entertainment Television ("BET") went public that I saw an African-American owned company go public. What's worst, when I left the SEC in 1998, I was unaware of any other African-American owned companies going public, and BET was in the process of delisting itself and becoming a private company again.

If we fast forward to today, much still looks the same in that there are only a handful of African-American owned public companies with Radio One, Inc. being the most well known. In my opinion, in order to be truly transformative, minority-owned companies must begin to rethink the concept of going public.

The threshold question any company should ask itself in analyzing the issue of going public is what are its pros and cons. Some of the benefits of going public include the following:

- **Cash** – A successful public offering can potentially yield a significant infusion of cash for the company, which can be used to accelerate its growth. This can be done through hiring more employees, building an infrastructure and producing better products and services.

- **Liquidity for employees** – As noted above, many companies structure stock incentive plans such that they can issue securities to employees and others as a means of further incentivizing them. When employees are issued these securities, they need to be put in the best position to sell some or all of their stock, if they so desire, in order to reap the rewards of their hard work. Going public is one mechanism that allows these employees to register and sell their stock on the open market.

- **Liquidity for Investors** – As I've been discussing throughout this book, investors want to maximize their returns and having one of their portfolio companies go public is a perfect way to do so.

- **Creation of a currency to pursue an acquisition strategy** – Once a company goes public it may desire to acquire another company or several companies and do so using its stock as currency. In this regard, the acquiring company might seek to acquire another company using stock and/or cash to purchase another company. For example, Company A wants to acquire Company B. Company A and Company B agree that the purchase price is $100. Company A may desire to pay cash; it may desire to pay Company B with $100 worth of Company A's stock or it may desire to pay Company B $50 cash and $50 worth of Company A's stock. The fact that Company A is a public company gives both parties more certainty as to the value of Company A's stock and gives Company B a level of comfort in knowing that the shares it receives from Company A pursuant to the transaction can be sold on the open market. As a result, an acquisition involving stock may be a bit more palatable to Company B.

- **Access to the capital markets for future financings** – As a public company, it now has the option of returning to the capital markets to raise cash. Depending upon the company's capitalization and existing market conditions, it can issue either equity or debt in order to meet its capital needs. Given that a company can raise substantially more money in the capital markets relative to the private market can be a tremendous weapon for a company in an increasingly competitive economy.

- **Enhances stature** – Being a public company can potentially enhance its stature and may benefit it in several ways, which include the following: (i) public companies generally receive more press coverage than private companies; (ii) customers may have the perception that public companies are more stable than private companies; (iii) creditors may be more inclined to provide favorable terms to a public company as opposed to a private company and (iv) public companies may appear more appealing to top management.

- **Enhanced market value** – As a general matter, private companies' valuations are more prone to a discount than public companies. In part, this is due to the fact that more information about public companies is available to the public and the fact that there is generally a broader investor base for public companies, which could increase the demand for a company's stock.

Some of the disadvantages of being a public company include the following:

- **Expensive** – Becoming a publicly traded company and maintaining your listing as a publicly traded company can be an expensive proposition. In order to become a publicly traded company, you can generally expect to pay the following fees: (i) SEC filing fees, (ii) exchange or Nasdaq filing fees, (iii) legal fees, (iv) accounting fees, (v) Blue-Sky fees and (vi) printing fees. As you can imagine, these fees can add up to be a fairly high number. Then, once becoming public, the company must meet its various regulatory and exchange related obligations. In particular, the company must file numerous reports with the SEC called periodic reports. These reports consist of the following: (i) the annual report on Form 10-K, (ii) the quarterly report on Form 10-Q, (iii) the current report on Form 8-K and (iv) the annual statement to all shareholders related to appropriate voting matters called the proxy statement. The cost to fully prepare and file these reports has always been a bit costly. However, upon passage of the Sarbanes Oxley Act of 2002 ("SOX"), the cost to prepare and file the periodic reports and proxy statement increased substantially. It's worth noting, however, that once it was determined that the costs publicly companies were incurring in order to comport with SOX was fairly substantial, the SEC passed rules to lessen the financial burden on smaller publicly traded companies.

- **Full Disclosure** – I recently had an opportunity to meet with an official of a securities exchange outside of the United States. This particular exchange did not have a substantial number of listed companies but it appeared to be well run and was looking for ways to incentivize more companies to consider going public. When I asked the official what he considered to be one of the biggest hurdles, his initial and immediate response was that of full disclosure. In other words, many companies in this particular country were reluctant to go public because they did not want to be subject to the full disclosure requirements of the countries' securities laws. This made me realize how I take this issue, the notion of full disclosure, for granted and perhaps it's because this is the underpinning of our philosophy under the federal securities laws. Specifically, the philosophy behind the Securities Exchange Act of 1934, which governs the filing of these periodic reports once a company goes public, is the theory that the more material information about a company that can be disseminated to the market, the better able the market is to make an informed judgment about that company. This is referred to as the efficient market theory. So, while full disclosure is a necessary evil, it can be viewed as burdensome by some.

- **Time Consuming** – In order to meet the various obligations of a public company, it demands that the company allocate an appropriate amount of resources towards the endeavor. Some companies are better equipped than others to handle this issue but it does require a substantial amount of time and resources to ensure that the company's obligations are being met.

- **Liability** – Among other things, a publicly traded company must comport with the federal securities laws. Failure to do so can result in the receipt of either a call or a letter from the SEC's Division of

Enforcement. Trust me when I say that you do not want this to happen.

Exchanges

Before attempting to go public, an analysis must first be performed to determine which exchange it should and can be listed on. As a general matter, companies primarily look at the New York Stock Exchange ("NYSE") and the Nasdaq Stock Market ("Nasdaq"). The NYSE is the world's largest stock exchange and Nasdaq is the largest electronic screen- based equity securities trading market in the United States. In order to apply for listing on either the NYSE or the Nasdaq, the company must first determine whether it meets their qualifications. It is also important to know that if a company does meet the qualifications of an exchange it wants to be listed on, it must continue to meet those listing qualifications once it becomes a publicly traded entity.

Underwriter

Choosing the correct underwriter to take a company public is a critical decision. Underwriters are investment banks that serve critical roles in the public offering process. Generally, the initial step an underwriter will take is a detailed due diligence analysis of the company. The underwriter will take this information and discern whether there is a public market for the company's securities. For starters, the underwriter will want to see the company's business plan and financial statements. If the business plan is deficient in any way, it will work with the company to develop a cohesive plan that will hopefully resonate with the investment community.

The underwriter will also review the financial statements. In this regard, they generally like to see that the company's financials are trending in the right direction and/or show long-term growth potential. The underwriter will also work diligently with the company's legal team to draft the disclosure document, which is referred to as a registration statement, which must be filed with the SEC and distributed to potential investors.

At the appropriate time, the underwriter will orchestrate and guide the company through a process known as a "road show," which is where the company gets to pitch the offering to potential investors. Finally, the underwriter facilitates the specific type of offering that is decided upon by the company and the underwriter, which is either a "firm commitment" or a "best efforts" offering. Both types of offerings will be discussed further below.

Finally, as a general matter, there are three primary factors a company considers in selecting an underwriter: (i) reputation, (ii) is it a regional or a national firm and (iii) whether the offering should be conducted as a firm commitment or a best efforts. The first factor is the underwriter's reputation. For example, does the underwriter have a good record of taking companies public? Has the underwriter taken companies public that are in the same space your company is in? Second, is the underwriter considered a regional or a national firm? It may be that for a particular offering, a regional underwriter is best in that the company does not have a national reputation but is very well regarded in one region of the country. In such instances, it may be beneficial to have a regional underwriter to take advantage of this type of situation. On the other hand, there are some offerings where it is imperative that the underwriters have a national reputation. This is often the case for larger offerings and for companies with a national reputation. Finally, it is important to consider the type of offering the company is likely to conduct. As noted above, there are two primary types of offerings: "firm commitment" and "best efforts." A firm commitment offering is one where the underwriter will commit to purchase 100% of the shares being offered and it will then sell the securities into the public market. A best efforts offering is where the underwriter will not commit to purchase any of the securities being offered by the company but will use its best efforts to find other investors to purchase them. As you can imagine, most companies want an underwriter that can handle a firm commitment offering but there are some instances where it is not feasible. For example, some underwriters are not large enough and/or do not have the infrastructure to support a firm commitment offering. Also, it may be determined that the offering is not strong enough for a firm commitment (i.e., the underwriters do not have enough confidence that once they purchase the company's securities they will be able to immediately sell such shares to the investment community).

Valuation

One of the more complex and negotiated aspects of a public offering is the valuation. That is, the company and the underwriters determine what it is worth at the time it goes public. This is important in that the valuation of the company will allow the parties to extrapolate how much of the company will have to be sold in order to raise the capital that is being sought. The factors that must be considered in this context are not dissimilar to what was discussed in relation to private offerings. The biggest distinction is that both the underwriter and the company have a vested interest in being as precise as possible. This is so because the last thing you want to have happen is to go public at, for example, $16.00 per share and the price immediately drops down to $10.00 per share. This scenario does happen on occasion for various reasons but it's not something anyone wants to see.

The Process

Thus far, we have discussed the components and the players associated with a public offering and set forth below are the steps in a public offering:

Step 1:   Internal Assessment.

The company must conduct its own internal analysis to discern whether it believes that going public is a viable option and whether it is in the company's long-term interest to do so. Many factors come into play here including the following:

- Is the equity market receptive to public offerings at this time?

- How have companies in your space faired in the public markets?

- Are the existing owners of the company willing to have their interests diluted?

- Has the company been performing well over the last few years?

- Is there anything on the horizon (e.g., material lawsuits, scandals, etc.) that can have a material adverse impact on the company?

- Does the company have the financial wherewithal to handle the initial costs associated with going public?

- Does the company need to consider making changes to its management team to make it more palatable to the public markets?

Step 2: Assemble the Team.

In addition to having a strong management team within the company, it must also look at developing an external team as well. The critical pieces of that team include the following:

- *Underwriters* – We discussed above the role of the underwriter and, as noted above, this is a critical decision.

- *Legal Counsel* – Irrespective of whether a company has internal counsel or a law firm that has represented it in the past, it is strongly recommended that the company consider retaining a law firm that has SEC experience.

- *Accounting Firm* – The federal securities laws require that the company's financial statements be audited. Just as with legal counsel, I think the same holds true in terms of the company utilizing

an accounting firm with significant SEC experience. This is especially so given the new rules
under SOX.

Step 3: Draft the Registration Statement

As noted above, the disclosure document used by
an issuer of securities to raise capital in the public markets is called a "registration statement." The contents
of a registration statement are dictated by the federal
securities laws and a failure to either fully disclose material information or the omission of material information
in the registration statement can result in civil and possibly criminal liability. Therefore, a significant amount
of time and energy is devoted to drafting a registration statement as it is intended to serve two primary
purposes: (i) provide information to potential investors
such that they can make an informed decision about
the securities being offered and (ii) protect the issuer in
that if it discloses all of the information it's suppose to,
the good, the bad and the ugly, then it has done all it
can do to make sure all material information has been
fully disclosed.

The registration statement contains both financial
and non-financial information including, but not limited to, the following: (i) a detailed business description,
(ii) the type of securities being offered, (iii) identifica-
tion of the management team and board of directors,
(iv) what the proceeds will be used for, (v) the risks associated with an investment in the company, (vi) a list of
the issuer's principal shareholders, (vii) management's
compensation and their compensation structure,
(viii) management's discussion and analysis of the issuer's

current financial picture and (ix) a description of any legal proceedings the issuer is involved in.

An entire team is used to properly draft a registration statement consisting of: management, attorneys, auditors and underwriters. Drafting the registration statement is a fairly detailed process as a mistake, in terms of what is disclosed or not disclosed and the wording of that disclosure, can potentially be the basis for a lawsuit. Therefore, the team is trying to make sure that the required information is disclosed and that it's accurately reflected in the registration statement.

Step 4: File Registration with the SEC/SEC Review Process

Now that the registration statement is completed, it can be filed with the SEC for review. It's important to note that the SEC does not review the registration statement to determine the merit of the offering. That is to say, the SEC does not review the offering for purposes of declaring whether this is either a good or a bad offering. Instead, the SEC reviews the offering to ensure that it includes all of the disclosure required by the federal securities laws such that a potential investor can review the document and is able to make an informed investment decision.

At the time the registration statement is filed, the issuer must file a registration fee with the SEC, which is based upon a formula set forth in the federal securities law. As you can imagine, the larger the offering the larger the fee.

Prior to the actual filing of the registration statement, the issuer must obtain certain codes such that at the time of filing, it is integrated into the SEC's online document system called Edgar. As a result, any time the issuer files the registration statement or an amendment to the registration statement with the SEC, such documents can be retrieved online by the public at www.sec.gov.

The registration statement is then forwarded to the appropriate branch ("Branch") within the Division of Corporation Finance, which is the transactional arm of the SEC. Each Branch is generally broken into industry groups. The Division's primary objective is to ensure that transactional documents contain proper disclosure such that shareholders are protected and to write rules under the Securities Act of 1933, as amended (the "Securities Act") and the Securities Exchange Act of 1934, as amended (the "Exchange Ac"). The registration statement is assigned to a team consisting of an attorney and an accountant. Both the accountant and the attorney will review the registration statement and draft comments that are integrated into what is called a "comment letter" that is sent to the issuer's counsel. As a general matter, it takes anywhere from 30-45 days for the SEC to review the registration statement and send out the comment letter.

For initial public offerings, these comment letters generally tend to be fairly extensive. Therefore, the issuer's team immediately begins to review the comment letter and begins the process of drafting a response to the comment letter and amending the registration statement accordingly. At such time as the issuer and its team are comfortable with the response letter and the amended registration statement, they are filed with the SEC. At this time, the review process at the

SEC begins again. However, for amendments, the SEC generally takes around 10 days to respond. This process continues until all of the issues raised by the SEC are addressed.

Step 5: Road Show

At such time as the issuer and its underwriters conclude that the registration statement is near completion, it begins the process of what is known as a "road show." During this time, the most recent version of the registration statement is printed for dissemination for prospective investors to review. Then, during a 1-2 week period, the lead investment bank along with the issuer's senior management, will make presentations to these potential investors, which are almost always institutional investors rather than individual investors. These meetings generally tend to be fairly intensive and a critical component of the offering process.

Step 6: Going Effective

If you look at the offering process as one big puzzle, then this next step is the final phase of the process where all of the pieces of the puzzle must come together. At this point, the following items, at a minimum, must be in place:

1. All of the SEC's comments have been addressed;

2. The underwriters have adequate belief that the market is conditioned such that the offering is well received by the public markets;

3. The underwriters and the issuer reach agreement on the issuer's valuation and

4. The exchange on which the issuer's securities will be traded is prepared to begin the process.

If the prerequisites referenced above are in place, then the issuer and the underwriters will agree on a date and time at which it wants the issuer's securities to begin trading. Once this date and time is set, issuer's counsel makes sure that ALL of the SEC's comments have been addressed and it submits what's called an acceleration letter to the SEC requesting that on a certain date and at a certain time, the SEC declares that the registration statement be declared "effective." By law, the acceleration request must be submitted to the SEC, by the issuer, 48 hours prior to the date the issuer seeks to have the registration statement declared effective. If a registration statement is declared effective by the SEC, it means that the issuer has addressed all of the issues raised by the SEC and it is cleared to become a public company.

The next 48 hours seem to take the longest as everything must be synchronized such that on the requested date and at the precise hour requested, the issuer's shares can begin trading. If anything goes wrong, it can spell disaster. What can possibly go wrong you might ask? Well, for starters, there is one more hurdle the issuer has to overcome, which is this. Once the issuer has submitted the acceleration request, the initial team of reviewers at the SEC packages all of the material it has in relation to the offering (e.g., correspondence between the SEC and the issuer, research material, internal memoranda, etc.) along with the final version of the registration statement. The material is submitted to the Branch's Assistant Director who must review it and sign off on the offering such that it is deemed effective. Remember, the acceleration request must be filed two days before the date the issuer and underwriters seek the have the registration statement declared effective. Therefore, the Assistant Director has two days to review all of the material, including the registration statement, and have any questions addressed by the team that is reviewing the filing. If there are issues and they are not adequately addressed before the time the issuer has requested to have its filing be declared effective, then there is a major problem. In those instances where there are such issues, the offering might end up being delayed and the underwriters generally assess its impact. Any delay in the offering can be perceived negatively by the market, which might adversely impact the offering. So, as you can see, this generally tends to be a stressful time for everyone involved. However, once all of these hurdles are cleared, and you see the issuer's stock symbol up and trading, it is an incredibly rewarding experience.

Mergers and Acquisitions

Another critically important exit event is a sale of the company. As I work with entrepreneurs who are considering raising capital, particularly those whose companies are at early stages of development, this concept tends to be the one they have the most trouble grasping. Not unlike the psychological hurdles that many entrepreneurs have to overcome before they realize the true benefits of raising capital and going public, the same holds true here. The refrain I usually here is this: "why would I want to sell something that I've put blood, sweat and tears into in order to make it success-ful. Don't you understand, this is my baby?" While this reaction makes perfect sense from a personal perspec-tive, it makes little sense from a business perspective.

The primary reason a company that has raised capi-tal can't eliminate the potential sale of the company is because once you take on shareholders (particularly those who have invested in your company), your fidu-ciary obligations extend not just to you but to your shareholders. So, if the circumstances are ripe at some point in the future for the company to be sold, the board, which presumably includes the founder, has a fiduciary obligation to give it fair consideration. Another reason this option should always remain on the table is that your objective as a business owner is to enhance value and grow wealth. Oftentimes, the business own-er's sole objective is to create a business institution that will provide such person with a source of income and such person can be the master of his or her fate. In such circumstances, it is likely that business owners with this mentality should not try to raise capital as the reality associated with raising capital is not aligned with such business owner's long-term view.

The primary problem with this mentality is this: in today's business environment, as I noted at the begin-ning of this book, entrepreneurs have to be transfor-mative in their way of thinking. This is particularly so as it relates to minority business owners. By this, I mean that, in today's environment, businesses need to be scalable, and the owners need to think in terms of growth. By definition, this means that business owners have to consider raising capital as it is the primary tool needed to meet this objective and if capital is raised, then you have to think in terms of exit events for your investors. If and when a business owner acknowledges and embraces this fundamental perspective, then the ability to accept the responsibilities that attach to it is much easier.

That being said, when exploring the sale of a company, there are two primary structures for consideration: (i) the sale of the company's assets and (ii) the sale of at least a majority of the company's stock.

The Process

Nondisclosure Agreement – This is a very important agreement between potential parties to a transaction. Essentially, the Nondisclosure Agreement ("NDA") sets forth the framework under which the parties can disclose information to one another with the understanding that there are legal consequences if a party discloses information in contravention of the agreement. In many instances, a client will provide me with an executed NDA it has obtained from some unknown source and, more often than not, the agreement is inadequate. Given the significance of the agreement, I strongly recommend that you have legal counsel either draft or review the NDA before executing the document.

Financial Due Diligence – Oftentimes, particularly for smaller transactions, you have a chicken or the egg issue when it comes to due diligence. On the one hand, you have a buyer who is interested in potentially making an offer to a potential target ("Target"). However, the Target doesn't want to waste its time and energy, unless it knows that the buyer is serious and has the financial wherewithal to consummate a transaction. The buyer, on the other hand, may be interested in making the offer and have the financial ability to consummate a transaction; however, it needs more information about the Target before a serious offer can be made. In these situations, the middle ground is to obtain financial information about the Target such that it can be reviewed and, if the buyer remains interested, it can then move forward with the term sheet and set forth a specific purchase price for the Target.

Term Sheet - As noted earlier, there are varying theories about whether parties to an acquisition transaction should begin with a term sheet. Transactions are all about leverage and some practitioners believe that the purchaser has greater leverage at the beginning of a transaction but loses some of that leverage if the term sheet is negotiated first. Be that as it may, the common approach is still to negotiate a term sheet as this gives both parties the ability to determine upfront, without putting in too much time and resource into the transaction, to determine whether this is something they want to move forward with. It should be noted that although term sheets are heavily negotiated, they are generally not binding agreements as both parties generally desire some flexibility as the transaction proceeds. The term sheet's primary components include, but are not limited to, the following:

a. *Purchased Assets or Stock*: Depending upon the type of transaction being negotiated, this section will set forth which assets will be purchased or the amount of stock that will be purchased pursuant to the transaction.

b. *Assumed Liabilities*: This section only applies if an asset transaction is being negotiated as it will indicate whether the purchaser will assume any liabilities and, if so, which liabilities will be assumed. If the transaction being negotiated is a stock transaction, then, as a general matter, the purchaser is assuming all of the Target's liabilities; therefore, such a discussion is not necessary.

c. *Purchase Price*: This section will detail how much will be paid for the Target and how it will be paid. For example, let's assume that the total purchase price is $1,000,000. However, instead of the purchaser bringing $1,000,000 cash to closing, the Target is willing to accept $500,000 cash at closing, then enter a promissory note with purchaser for the remaining $500,000. All of this would have to be described in the term sheet such that both parties have a clear understanding of the transaction's structure.

d. *Due Diligence*: This section will generally indicate that the potential purchaser will have the right to perform due diligence on the Target. It will outline the parameters that both parties must comport with in relation to the due diligence and the amount of time during which it can be performed.

e. *Exclusivity*: The wording of this section tends to be heavily negotiated because of its significance.

The section generally provides that for a certain agreed upon period of time, the Target will not shop or enter similar term sheets with other potential purchasers. As these transactions tend to be not only time consuming but also costly, the potential purchaser seeks to ensure that its time and money will not be wasted at no fault of its own.

f. *Contingencies*: This section sets forth the conditions and circumstances under which either party can cease moving forward on the transaction. For example, this section might provide that if the potential purchaser doesn't like what it sees during the course of due diligence it can cease moving forward on the transaction. Another example is a financial contingency, which might provide that the potential purchaser needs to either raise or borrow some of the funds needed to consummate the transaction; however, if it is unable to do so then it is not obligated to move forward with the transaction.

Due Diligence – Performing due diligence is a critical component of the transaction. This gives the potential purchaser a first-hand look at the Target's operations. To begin the due diligence process, the potential purchaser will generally forward a very detailed due diligence checklist, which will set forth a request for specific items including: contracts, permits, insurance, taxes and so forth. Based upon this information, the potential purchaser, as well as its legal counsel, can make certain assessments about the Target and draft the definitive agreements accordingly.

Definitive Agreements – Depending upon the type of transaction the parties have agreed upon and the agreed upon items in the term sheet, the parties will begin drafting the appropriate definitive purchase agreements along with all appropriate ancillary agreements. For example, it is not uncommon in an asset transaction for the parties to agree in the term sheet that not only will the purchaser acquire assets but it will also hire certain individuals who work with the Targets, generally the founders, as either employees or consultants. Therefore, the parties will also draft either employment agreements or consulting agreements as appropriate. At the end of the day, however, it is not until such time as the definitive agreements are signed is the transaction consummated.

Asset Sale

As a general matter, buyer's seek to structure the transaction as an asset deal, as opposed to a stock deal, because of the following: (i) the buyer has the opportunity to select which assets it wants to acquire; (ii) the buyer can negotiate which liabilities, if any, it is willing to assume and (iii) perhaps most importantly, the buyer is generally entitled to a stepped-up basis in the assets, which is favorable from a tax perspective (i.e., a readjustment of the appreciated value of an asset for tax purposes).

Stock Sale

Just as asset deals are favored among purchasers, stock deals are favored among Targets. The reason a potential Target favors a stock transaction is that the buyer takes on the existing liabilities as well. Sellers have many motivations for wanting to sell a company and the ability to shed itself of existing liabilities is oftentimes a primary reason. Just as with an asset deal, a stock transaction can be structured in a variety of ways. For example, the potential purchaser can acquire 100% of the Target's stock. Another alternative is for the potential purchaser to acquire a majority of the Target's stock and allow certain persons, generally the founders of the company, to retain the remaining amount of stock. The idea here is that those who have been able to retain some of the Target's stock will continue to work for the company for some agreed upon period of time and be incentivized to work as hard as possible to make the company grow such that they can then sell those shares, presumably to the purchaser, at a higher valuation in the future.

Private Equity Funds

Much of the impetus behind the merger and acquisition market can be directly attributed to the private equity market. Similar to venture capital funds, private equity funds ("P/E Funds") raise large sums of capital except that they focus solely on acquiring the company or, at a minimum, a controlling interest. P/E Funds then either bring on their own management teams or work directly with current management to position the company for a successful exit event. The other distinguishing factor of a P/E Fund, relative to a venture capital fund, is it generally utilizes debt and cash to fund its acquisitions.

P/E Funds generally use a multiple of earnings before interest taxes depreciation and amortization ("EBITDA") in determining the acquisition purchase price. For example, if Company A has an EBITDA of $1,000,000, the P/E Fund may use a multiple of 5x and make an offer of $5,000,000. The multiple used by the P/E Fund is generally dependent upon the Target's industry. Finally, as a general matter, P/E Funds tend to look for exit events via either IPO or sale of the company.

CHAPTER 7

Conclusion

As I noted at the outset, this book is intended to give you a snapshot of the financing life cycle and some of the issues you should be cognizant of as a minority-owned company. The key takeaway from this book is that there is a method to the madness. There are entry points and exit points for every company, but you must be armed and ready to aggressively move forward if you want to maximize the capital you can generate. In other words, before you can operate efficiently in this system, you must first know how all of the components operate and develop a strategy with respect to how you intend to make it a successful venture.

Raising capital is not for every business owner and it's not for every business. You first have to sort out in your mind what your goals are in relation to your company. If you essentially want a lifestyle company, more likely than not, you shouldn't try and raise capital. If your company is scalable and truly has the potential to grow with the right resources, then you should consider raising capital.

Having the right team around you is critical. This entails not only a strong management team but a strong team of advisors as well: namely an attorney and an accountant. I remember during the technology boom, an accountant in the city was known for preparing companies to go public. Over the span of two years, I worked on two initial public offerings where he was chief financial officer for each company. In other words, he took Company A public then after his options vested he moved on to Company B and did the same thing. I suspect he continued to do this until the end of the tech boom. You don't see this going on today but the point is there are service providers that know the ropes and have the relationships that are necessary to help you navigate your way through the financial life cycle.

So, trust yourself, trust the system and let's make some deals happen.

Good luck!